DATE DUE

MAY 18 1997	
UPI 261-2505	PRINTED IN U.S.A.

FiREFLiES iN THE NiGHT

BY
Judy Hawes

Illustrated
BY
**KAZUE
MIZUMURA**

FIREFLIES IN THE NIGHT

Thomas Y. Crowell
COMPANY
NEW YORK

LET'S-READ-AND-FIND-OUT BOOKS

Special Adviser: *DR. ROMA GANS*, Professor Emeritus of Childhood Education, Teachers College, Columbia University.

Editor: *DR. FRANKLYN M. BRANLEY*, Coordinator of Educational Services, American Museum—Hayden Planetarium, consultant on science in elementary education.

Air Is All Around You
Animals in Winter
Bees and Beelines
The Big Dipper
Big Tracks, Little Tracks
Birds Eat and Eat and Eat
The Clean Brook
Down Come the Leaves
Find Out by Touching
Fireflies in the Night
Flash, Crash, Rumble, and Roll
Follow Your Nose
How a Seed Grows

How Many Teeth?
Icebergs
In the Night
It's Nesting Time
The Listening Walk
Look at Your Eyes
The Moon Seems to Change
My Five Senses
My Hands
Rain and Hail
Rockets and Satellites
Sandpipers

Seeds by Wind and Water
Snow Is Falling
Spider Silk
Starfish
The Sun: Our Nearest Star
A Tree Is a Plant
Upstairs and Downstairs
Watch Honeybees with Me
What Makes a Shadow?
What Makes Day and Night
What the Moon Is Like
Where the Brook Begins
The Wonder of Stones

2   3   4   5   6   7   8   9   10

FIREFLIES IN THE NIGHT

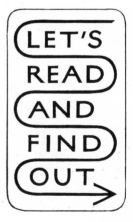

LET'S
READ
AND
FIND
OUT

I like fireflies. When I visit my grandfather in the summer-
time, we sit outdoors after supper and watch them.

Grandmother likes to watch them too. She calls them lightning
bugs. They look like little dancing stars. They are really
beetles, grandfather says.

Their front wings are hard and their back wings are soft.
They live in the ground most of the time.

Grandfather gave me a glass jar to take on firefly hunts. We punched holes in the lid.

Fireflies are easy to catch and soon my jar is lighted up like a lantern.

After every firefly hunt, grandfather has something new to tell me. One time he told me how to make my firefly lantern brighter. Just hold the jar upright in a bowl of warm water.

He knew it would work because fireflies always shine brighter
    in warm weather.
If you dip the jar in cold water, the firefly lights will fade.

People in hot countries use fireflies more than we do. The men there wear net bags full of fireflies tied to their ankles. These homemade flashlights help men find their way along the dark jungle paths.

Grandfather let me try this in the cornfield,
because we have no jungle.

In Japan, the gardens are lighted at night by firefly lanterns.
That must be nice!

Grandfather told me about a doctor in Cuba who, many years ago, once used a firefly lamp in his operating room. His other lights had gone out!

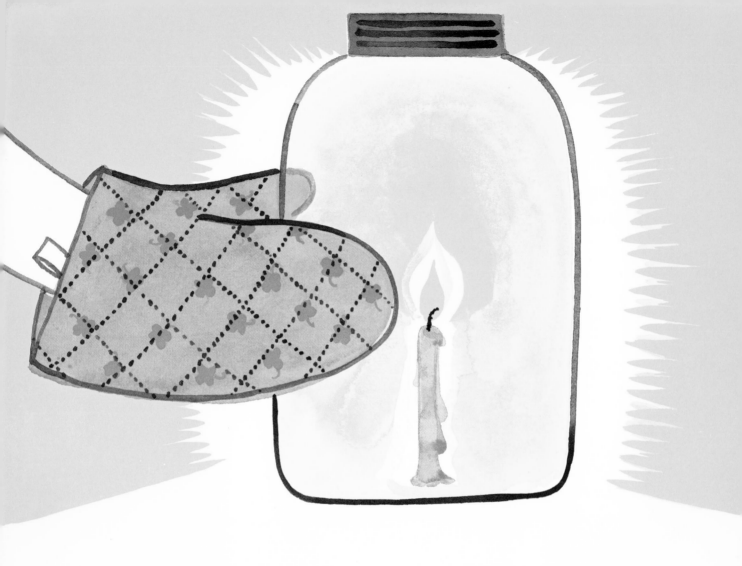

Fireflies make *cold* light. Candles make hot light. If I put one tiny birthday candle in a jar, the jar gets too hot to hold.

My firefly lantern never gets warm.

I asked my grandfather, "How is it that fireflies can make cold light?"

He told me that it is because fireflies have chemicals inside them called luCIFerin and luCIFerase. When fireflies take in air, the air mixes with these chemicals. Flash!—the mixture makes light *without heat*.

Small holes on the side of the firefly let air in.

Luciferin and luciferase mix with air in the underpart of the firefly.

Luciferin and luciferase plus air equals cold light.

Some day I will learn more about luciferin and luciferase.

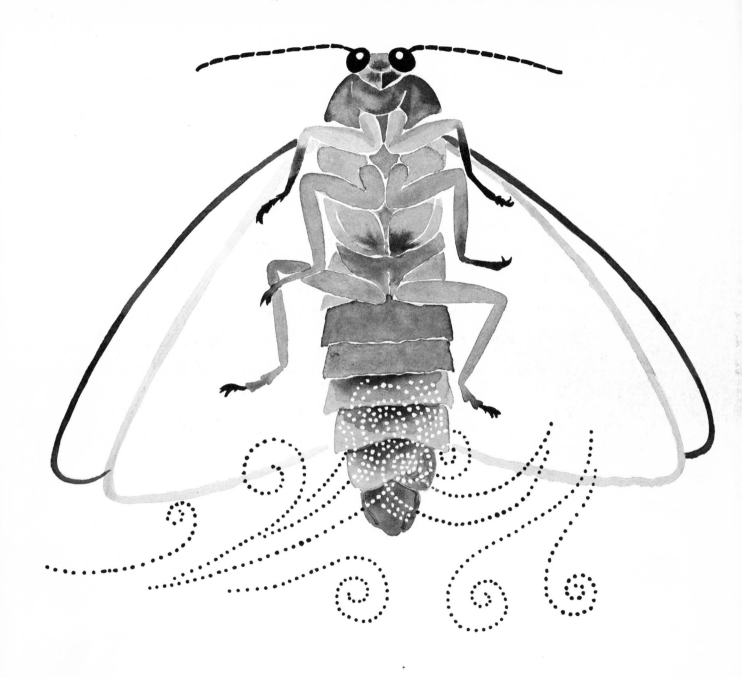

Fireflies flash the same light signal over and over again. As he
flies around, the male firefly may make a signal like this:

3 or 4 or 5 quick flashes.

Wait for 6 seconds.

Repeat.

The female firefly stays in the grass and gives her own kind of
answering signal, probably like this:
       1, 2, or 3 quick flashes.
       Wait for 2 seconds.
       Repeat.
That's how fireflies find their mates.

Grandfather says if I sit quietly in the grass and flash a small
flashlight on and off every two seconds, the fireflies may be
fooled and come to *me*!
I am going to try that tomorrow night.

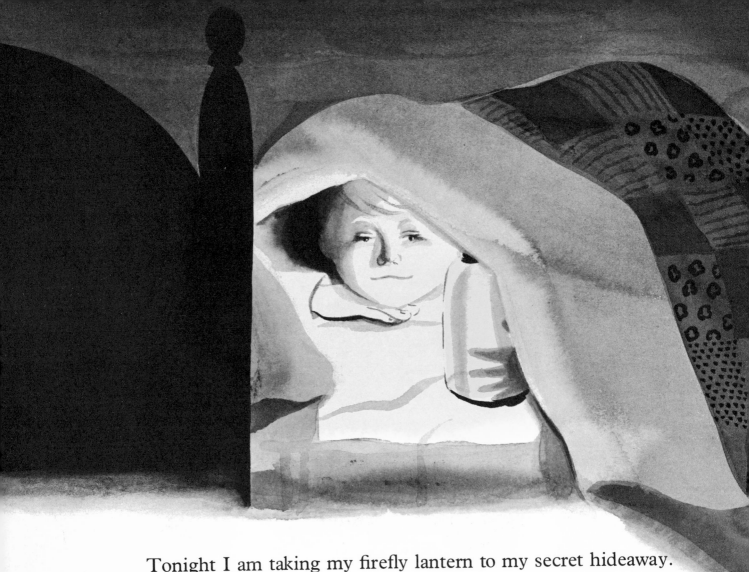

Tonight I am taking my firefly lantern to my secret hideaway.
Under the bedcovers my lantern makes a cozy light.
Just for me!

My grandmother will come soon to say goodnight.
"Lights out," she will say. She will take my lantern outside
   and let my fireflies go.

I'll catch some more tomorrow night.

ABOUT THE AUTHOR

Mrs. Hawes's busy life includes teaching in a New Jersey public school, working with girl scouts, and teaching Sunday school. A native of Forest Hills, New York, she received an A.B. degree from Vassar College and studied at Paterson State College and Newark State College. Mrs. Hawes lives in Glen Rock, New Jersey, with her husband and four children.

ABOUT THE ILLUSTRATOR

Miss Mizumura is well known as an illustrator and jacket artist for both children's and adult books. Her busy life also includes textile design, advertising layout, and Japanese brushdrawing.

Kazue Mizumura was born in Kamakura, Japan. She studied at the Gakushuin (Peeresses' School) and the Women's Art Institute in Tokyo, as well as at Pratt Institute in Brooklyn, New York. Miss Mizumura lives in New York City.